# She Still Rises

## The Continuing Journey of
## Muletta Hayes

Written By
## Deaconess Muletta Hayes

R.D. Talley Books
Bookstore & Publishing

www.rdtalleybooks.com

Las Vegas, Nevada

ISBN: 978-1-957294-11-7

R.D. Talley Books Publishing, LLC
4882 W. Lone Mountain Road
Las Vegas, Nevada 89130
www.rdtalleybooks.com

# Preface

I decided to write this book because everyone has a story to tell. I wanted to share mine and I did not write it for sympathy or to point anyone out. I chose pieces of my life to show that even though sometimes the road is rough and you feel as though you cannot make it, God WILL step in. Please know that I did not use anyone's real names so I can protect myself at all costs. The only names I did use were my husband's, children and grandchildren, and that is only because if they sued me, they would only get what they would have gotten after my demise…practically nothing.

I did not mention each and every person that was in my life. People come into your life for a reason, a season and or a lifetime. I chose to use lifetime people who affected me in some type of way or another. The lessons I've learned through seasonal people was just that…a lesson. So please don't be offended if you don't see your name or someone close to your name. I still love everyone who was and still is a part of my life, but this book is to highlight my journey.

The journey through life is filled with wonder, challenges, broken hearts, highs and lows, celebrations, special moments and memories that define us. It is these events, planned or unexpected, that impact our travel and define our purpose. I wanted to include all who were part of that. Thank you for understanding. May God continue to bless you and keep you.

# Contents

## **Bonus Poems/Material**

# 1 | Mrs. Hattie B (Mother)

I was born on December 30th, 1968. Yes, I'm a winter baby, which explains why I love the cold weather so much. The first few years of my life seemed like a blur...I don't remember much about my young childhood, but I do remember HER...Mrs. Hattie Bernice King...my mother. She was the baby of eleven children born to my grandparents Ben and Lillie Graham. We lived in Newark, New Jersey in a small house on the second floor. My room was adjacent to her bedroom. When I close my eyes, I can still see the windows in the front. They were three panels uniquely curved. From the second floor, it looked scary looking down outside of them.

Because I was so very young, some of the memories that I have are vague and some of them seem like a dream. According to some of my older cousins, my mother was a loving mother, sister, aunt and friend. She was sort of a jokester. Now I see where I get that from (smile). She always wore a smile whenever you saw her, even through her pain.

My mother named me Muletta King. I don't know where she got the name "Muletta" from. I was told that it meant "little bad one". The King part came from her ex-husband whom she was married to. Later in my life I found out that he was just a name on my birth certificate. Why did she do that?? I have no idea. I found my biological father when I was around 15 or 16 years old. I will tell you about that later.

I remember how she used to do my hair in the mornings before school and how she would play in it and we would laugh. I can still hear her laughter. Sometimes she would allow me to stay home because no one would know. My older siblings, Wennie and Paddy, left before I did and came home later than I did. I loved it. The quality time that we spent together was priceless, and even though I was young, I knew that she enjoyed it as much as I did.

My mother gave birth to three beautiful girls and one handsome son. I was what they called back then, "the knee baby." That meant I was right before the youngest baby. My older sister, Wennie, was five years older than me, my brother, Paddy, was four years older than me and my little sister, Kesah is five years younger than me.

We had different fathers except the oldest two. They had the same dad. I remember sometimes when their dad would stop by, my mom would let him have it! Apparently, he was not doing his job as a father. I sort of felt sorry for him. I don't remember ever needing something and didn't have it. My mother loved us more than we knew and she made sure we had what we needed.

My mom's "special friend" stayed with us. He was my baby sister's father, Arnie. He was very nice and very kind. He was from Haiti…very handsome. He loved her children. He and my mom encouraged me to play the piano. I took lessons but I did not like them…they were too hard and unfortunately, my patience was very thin. I learned a wee bit, just enough to say that I knew a song or two. Although it was not very much, it was just enough for her. My mother was very proud of me. Every time we had company she would say, "Go play your song on the piano Muletta." Yes of course, I obliged. I was happy that I had made her proud. My mother had courage and strength. She was determined and she wanted the best for her children. Although trials came throughout her life, she never let them deter her from protecting her kids.

In November of 1976, she became very sick and made arrangements for us as she fought her battle. We were all sitting on her bed, and she asked us 'if something were to happen to her, where would we like to go?' Wennie and

Paddy said with their father. I replied the same but my mom asked me 'wouldn't I like it better to stay with my Aunt Tilda? That way I can play with my cousin, Atina, who was about my age.' I excitedly said yes, not knowing what was really going on. I know now that the reason why she did that was because she knew that he was not my biological father. I remember it as if it were yesterday. I was only seven years old at the time. Wennie and Paddy stayed with their father. I stayed with Aunt Tilda and my baby sister, Kesah, stayed with her father, who was already at the home.

My mother was diagnosed with Cancer of the Cervix and Uterus in 1974. Back then, they did not have the technology that they have today. My mother had decided to take a trip to North Carolina after her diagnosis. She asked one of my older cousins to drive her. He said yes. The only one of her children she took was me. She was coming home to say her goodbyes to her mom and dad, my grandparents. She knew how far she was in her sickness and knew that she did not have a lot of time. She also knew that they were not going to travel to New Jersey. Once back home, she visited family members and old friends. Little did they all know that would be their last time seeing her.

She continued to fight this battle, and unfortunately lost on December 1st, 1976 at 4:20 a.m. It was a cold Wednesday morning and snow was on the ground. By that time, I was already staying with my Aunt Tilda. That cold December morning, one of my other aunts came into the room with a friend of the family as I was getting dressed for school. She asked if I knew the meaning of the word "death". I nodded my head yes. She continued in a crackly voice to explain that my mother was no longer with us. With tears rolling down my face, I continued to put my boots on for school. As I was leaving out the door to head for school, I noticed a few people in the living room…my aunts and my sister and brother's dad. They were making burial arrangements for my mother. My whole morning was very emotional and I did not need to be at school in the first place. Needless to say, my attendance at school that day was very short.

My mother was buried in an aqua chiffon dress. She looked so at peace, as if she was sleeping. As a matter of fact, Kesah, who was three at the time, was greeting people at the door asking them if they want to see her mommy…she was sleeping. I remember while I was looking at her, it appeared to be a tear rolling down her cheek from her right eye. I know now that it was a part of the defrosting, but I still say a tear because she didn't want to leave us. Jesus loves the little children.

*"God knew the road was getting rough*
*The hills were hard to climb,*
*He gently closed her loving eyes*
*And whispered, 'Peace Be Thine.'"*

# *In Loving Memory of Mrs. Hattie Bernice King*

When I think about my mother,
I can't help but to stop for a while
I remember all the times we shared
that made me laugh and smile

I think of how she had took her time
and hugged me every day,
How she looked into my eyes
when there were no words to say

I think about getting ready for school
as she did my hair,
Cooking dinner when I came home…
she was always there

My mother had to go for a while,
so God stepped in for me
To make sure I was taken care of
by friends and family

He wiped away the tears I wept,

the pain, he took it too

But memories he left deep inside

for difficult times to get through


Although she is no longer in sight

I know in time I will see

That she never really left,

she is forever with me


So, on this special day

although my heart is tore

I will celebrate her life, love and laughter

knowing I love her...but God loved her more.

# 2 | Let's Grow Up

I started staying with my Aunt Tilda that November before my mom passed away. I used to go to her house when my mom was really sick, mostly after her chemo. This time it was for good. My aunt and uncle were not rich, but they were well to do. My uncle was a hardworking man who loved his family. Although he was very quiet, you knew he loved you. My Aunt Tilda was a meek and humble woman who loved her family. They also lived in Newark, New Jersey in a two-family house. We were on the second floor with a balcony built in, and it had three bedrooms.

They had three girls of their own…Vonnie, Lyn and Atina. Atina was eight months younger than me. When I moved in, Vonnie was already out of the house and Lyn was in high school. I was very grateful they opened their door for me. Atina and I shared the same room until Lyn went off to college. I remember Atina and I used to use our beds as houses and play with our barbies all day long. We had very vivid imaginations. Washcloths as bedding, spools of thread as seats, jewelry boxes as tables or dressers and let's not forget the thimble as a cup. Yes, we argued, but to me, she was more than just my cousin. She was my sister/cousin. All three of them were, and still are my sister/cousins.

One time we were in the bathroom calling ourselves 'about to be' blood sisters. We grabbed one of my uncles razor blades and I was supposed to just do a thin slice on her thumb and mine. I made a mistake and did a nick instead. She was bleeding and started to cry. I took the razor and nicked myself too. I didn't want her to hurt or cry. My sister first, my cousin last, my friend, always.

Because I stayed with my mother's sister, I got to see my family regularly, especially my grandparents who lived in North Carolina. I got to see my aunts and uncles on my mom's side of the family very often. My mother was very close to her family but even closer to two of her sisters, so we were more than just cousins. One of my other aunts, Aunt Helma, was responsible for me as well…she's my 3rd mom. She is partly responsible for the woman that I am today. I'm glad I turned out okay…I'm just saying. She is also where I get my sassiness from.

I have this male cousin that used to come over all the time, her son of course, Wayen. We used to go over to his house as well. Me, him and Atina called ourselves,

"The Graham Crackers." All of our mothers were sisters and their maiden name was Graham. We sound like a singing group Lol. We were anything but. I know I couldn't hold a note even if it had a handle on it.

I also got to see and visit with my sisters and my brother. My stepfather, Arnie, would come and pick me up so that I could spend the weekend with Kesah. One fond and exciting memory I can recall is around Christmas one year. I do believe I was about eight years old going on nine. Atina and I were looking for something in the basement of our house. Being nosey. We ran across a small room, so we opened the door. See, I told you, nosey. In the room we saw so many toys and stuff. I told her, "Hey, there is that doll you asked Santa for." She said, "and there is that game that was on your list!" Yep, you guessed it!! That was the year that we both discovered there was no Santa. Yikes! I guess you can say spoiler alert. Nosey-behind kids. Yep, that's us!

After living in Newark for a while, in 1982, we moved to Roselle, New Jersey. Roselle was a quiet suburban area. We were so excited!! Moving out of the city into the suburbs…a beautiful new house with three bedrooms and a nice sized basement…not to mention a big backyard. Atina and I both had our own rooms. I was 13 years old, about to start high school. I was excited about meeting new people and going to a nice school. We had a mirror on our wall in our dining room, which was the same mirror from the living room of our home in Newark. I loved that mirror. It made the room appear to be bigger than what it was. I even wrote a poem about it. Later that summer, we added a pool in the backyard…Splash Party!! It was hard work, but my cousins and I had fun putting it up. Much of my time was spent in the basement though. I loved going down there and playing my records and singing. I basically escaped to our basement.

On the first day of school, I was really nervous and was very unsure of myself. I was a bit on the heavy side but that never stopped me from being me. But to me, this was different. I was, and still am very outgoing, however on this particular day, I felt like I was walking them long halls completely naked. Can you imagine? Nope, don't do it to yourself. After going from class to class and meeting my new teachers and students, I really liked this school. I felt that I fitted in. By the end of the day, it had totally turned around. I met a few people and felt more at ease.

That freshman year went by so quick. Summer was here already. This was the summer that I began writing poetry. I found it as a way to escape and to express myself, so I would lose myself in my writing sometimes. I had no idea at that time that it was a gift. A precious gift from God. I acquired the gift of ministering through poetry. I know now that some people relate better to listening to poetry or song. I cherish it and I don't take it for granted.

I also met a guy from school. He was a year older than I was and we called ourselves dating. He was very nice and very sweet but also very experienced. We sat on my front porch for hours and just talked. I remember one time I went over to his house…that was the day he showed me he was way more experienced than I was. No…we didn't do the nasty! I am not that kind of girl. I asked him to walk me home and he did. The shortest relationship ever in history. We remained friends until he graduated but lost contact after that. Throughout the rest of my high school years I've made friends, lost friends and grew up a bit. I considered myself to be a very happy and content young lady.

When I was around 15, one evening, Vonnie's friend came by the house. She worked for Social Services. What county?? I have no idea, but she said this little light-skinned man came in and asked about Muletta McCoy. Since Muletta was a very rare name, the only one she could think of was me. Low and behold, it was my biological father looking for me. Would you believe that?! We found his number, so I built up the nerve and called him. When I finally met him face to face, I realized how much I resembled him. A whole lot fell into place, especially my love for poetry. I found out that I had a whole family on my father's side. I also found out that he was 25 years older than my mother. I only spoke to him on the phone mostly. His favorite place to go to was Atlantic City. I didn't get too many opportunities to go. To this day, I have never been. I did get to go with him to his home in Newark and meet some of my siblings.

Everyone has that special someone that they were with during high school. I am not exempt from that. I had a special him too. I met him during the summer between my sophomore and junior year. I was just finding out who Muletta was, and I was friends with his sister. When we first met, it was like 'Meh!' Whatever! But as we got to know each other, we became closer friends. During this time, I had what you may call a boyfriend. He was in a grade under me…but of course that did not stop me from being friends with old boy. No, I am not that kind of girl… we were just friends. As a matter of fact, we all went to the junior prom together. Unfortunately, my newfound friend and his date were dismissed from the prom because she brought alcohol to the event. Smart chic huh? Anyway, that summer, my boyfriend and I broke up and me and my newfound friend started dating.

Muletta and Rus became an item. What kind of item? Heck if I know. He was a very sweet guy and I really did have feelings for him. We dated for our junior year and then we mutually decided that we were better-off as friends. As boyfriend and girlfriend, we did not get along very well. I was a flirt and he wasn't having it. Plus, to be completely honest, it was our senior year boo boo!! I did NOT want to be tied down to one particular guy. I wanted freedom to go to any event without extra luggage (if you get what I mean).

I had joined this rapping group who were just a bunch of guys from my school and we used to hit it at house parties and such. That's when I got my nickname: Mu-Ski. Yeah, that's really corny…but it wasn't back in the day. Sike…yes it was. I didn't know it back then, but my rapping and poetry was basically the same thing. Just one is to music and the other is to a heart. I used to play my favorite group all the time in our basement…Sugar Hill Gang. But any who, to this day, Rus and I still remain friends. We have seen each other through both our first marriages and other people in our lives. I have even made him the God-father of my daughter. Although breaking up was a little bit hurtful at the time, I am glad we did because I don't know whether or not we would have remained friends had we broken-up differently.

My high school years were so complex. I mean, some days I was so happy and other days I was severely depressed. It was not normal teenage stuff. My mind raced all the time and most of the time I had no idea who I was. No one had any idea the war I was going through or the battles I was fighting within myself. I didn't feel worthy of anything and felt completely lost. I was emotionally exhausted. The sad part is that I had no one I could talk to…or should I say, I felt there was no one who would listen. I kept these feelings bottled up inside for a long time…I mean, they are just being surfaced now.

I was scared and missed my mom like crazy. Although my aunt was there, there is no one like your mom. She missed everything. I was so mad at her for leaving me. I was alone and lonely in the midst of a crowd. So, I just lived-up to the reputation that fat people are always jolly and never even showed any of the emotions I was going through. I believe that was my first mistake.

By bottling up my feelings, I allowed all of my worries, fears, doubts, anger and depression build up to this gigantic monster that apparently takes over from time to time. God, I need you!

# Graham Crackers

Never has there been
any cousins closer than we
hanging together all the time
just us three

We would play all day
and in between fuss and fight
but when darkness fell outside
we'd ask, 'could we spend the night?'

I remember that time
when we ran from that dog
the baby graham cracker got bit
and we jumped up like a frog

Our mothers were all sisters
and we felt just as close
of all the other cousins
we loved each other the most

As time passed us by
we went a different direction
even time and distance did not interfere
with our love and affection

We're still just as close
as close as can be
The famous Graham Crackers
Atina, Wayen and Me.

# Reflections

For as long as I can remember,
and as clear as I can recall
Mama's mirror has been in our family
carefully placed against the wall

If this mirror could only speak
it would have lots of stories to convey
Some of them happy, some of them sad,
the memories we thought just faded away

It could tell you about the Christmases,
the love and laughter we shared
It would tell you about how arms were opened
and a family who showed they cared

It will tell you about Vonnie
who checked herself once or twice
Checking to make sure she was decent
and her clothes fit on her nice

It would tell you about Lyn
who stares at herself as she speaks,
Admiring her beauty she possess
being humble and meek

It would tell you about Atina
who loved to look at herself while on the phone
Whom with Muletta danced and sang to
when no one was at home

It would tell you about Muletta
the cousin of the crew
Who practically lived in it
but mostly her hair she would do

It would tell you about the conversations
it recorded when we were in high school
The girlfriends we had over
and the boyfriends who thought they were cool

It would speak of the hard times,
the sickness, the aches and the tears
All the tribulations
our family endured over the years

But most of all, it would tell you
how in any kind of weather
We cried, we laughed,
and through it all, we stuck together

It now sees the grandchildren,
the Thanksgivings filled with love
The blessings upon the Smith family
by the good Lord above

Thank you, Lord,
for this mirror that you placed upon our wall
Trying to live right so in it what we'll see
is a reflection of you most of all.

# 3 | What in the World is Job Corps?

Graduation came and went, and the days went by so fast. Both of my maternal aunts were so happy and proud. They literally cried. I cried too. I am sure that they wished my mom could have witnessed me walking across that stage. I know I did.

I tried to go to a local college, but that didn't work. It seems that I did not know what I was doing when I filled out my paperwork. I wanted to learn how to work a computer, not learn how a computer works. So, I dropped out before the first semester even ended. To be completely honest, I only attended because a friend of mine was going there too. Talk about your peer pressure.

Now, here I am not in college anymore and have no idea what life even has to offer. I did not want to just sit around and twiddle my thumbs together. There was literally nothing for me to do in Roselle. I eventually became too big for my britches and wanted to move out of my aunt's house. I called my sister, Wennie. I packed my bags and went to the front door and waited for her to come and pick me up. At this time, neither my aunt nor my uncle was home. The only one that was there was Atina. She sat on the floor watching tv the whole time I packed. When I went to the front door, she didn't move a muscle, nor did she say a word. Wennie pulled up and I headed to the car. Something told me to look back and I did. There was Atina watching me from the window as I left. I never in a million years wanted to ever hurt her. I believe that day I honestly did. Just to see her look on her face, my heart went into my stomach, but I knew there was no turning back now. I regret that.

My crazy self moved in with Wennie. She and her husband lived in an apartment in South Jersey. Can someone say "mistake"?? It should have come with a warning. They were so adamant about me getting a job. It's not like I wasn't trying. I did try. I guess I wasn't trying hard enough, so they insisted I join a job corps. Wennie had no idea what that was. She was just listening to what people were telling her. She must have figured to herself, 'Oh…a job…plus a trade and an allowance. You can't beat that?' Yes, you can…and with a hammer!!…DUH

My journey now began at a Job Corps in New Jersey. For those of you who do not know what Job Corps is, it is a place to go if you have nothing to lean on in life.

They give you free room and board and teach you a trade. You live on the premises that resemble barracks in the military. You share a room with as little as two people or as many as five. I did not like this place at all. They gave us an allowance every weekend. We were allowed to leave for the weekends and go home or visit but had to be back by Sunday at a certain time. I used to catch the train to Aunt Tilda's house and visit. I missed being at home with them, but like I said, I knew it was too late for me to turn back. Little did I know that this would be the place where I'd meet my first husband. Did I say already that I did not like this place at all?? Well, let me say that again!! I did not like this place at all!

Since there was nowhere else for me to go, I figured I would make the best of a bad situation. I would give this a try and see how it goes. We had classes, we had chores and we had minimal freedom. Well…at least I tried. Oh, we did have movie night. That was when we all got together and sat in the gym and watched a movie on a big screen. That was the first time I saw Howard the Duck. Good movie, by the way. My "boyfriend" was very demanding, obsessive and loud. Did I view that as a warning? Nope! Somebody get her head checked! I plead the blood over my life.

# 4 | My Coma Years

I am just going to keep this part of my book simple and to the point because if I don't, I will allow myself to go down what I consider to be an emotional roller coaster. Besides, it took me quite a while to put this behind me. At first, I was not going to mention this at all, but I eventually decided to include it. And that is only because I believe that it will help or bless someone. I call these my coma years because it seemed like I was in a coma. I was away from my family and friends and barely had any contact with them. I was alone and desolate. I felt lonely and was quite depressed. So, here we go. All aboard this roller coaster. Please keep all arms and legs inside the vehicle at all times.

My first husband was…how can I put this…poison flavored as your favorite drink. I was with him for two years and I consider those to be my coma years. I was out of touch with my family and friends, not because I wanted to be, but because of him. The treatment that I endured throughout our marriage was nothing but torture. He knew what buttons to press. He was abusive and manipulative.

He threatened my family through me, therefore I was scared to leave.

I met him while I was participating in Job Corps. When I first saw him, he was with another girl. I paid no mind to him, but of course that relationship did not last. We started talking and there you have it. Before I knew it, we were a couple. A couple of idiots if you asked me, but back then you could not tell me anything. The last girl he was with tried to warn me of his anger issues, but of course I ignored her. Why in the world did I do that? Soon, I was pregnant with his child. Because I was pregnant, they moved me from the big dorm, where there were six girls to a room, to the little dorm. It was just me and another girl in the same room.

At the beginning, he was sweet and loving. When we got married, I was 18 and he was 21. The anger within him would show its ugly head ever so often but I brushed it off to having a bad day. Yeah…little did I know. I was so naive. Holding down a job was a challenge, so we struggled immensely to the point we were sleeping in a car, on people's floors and in strange places. We ate at food pantries and sometimes I wore the same clothes three days in a row. It never crossed my little tedious mind to JUST GO HOME!

As I am writing this, I realize now how immature and stupid I really was. Over time, the anger was escalating but by then I saw no way out. I felt stuck and now scared. He became more erratic every day passing and it affected me and my baby. Now here comes DYFS!...Department of Youth and Family Services. My husband's temper blew up so much that now she and I both have bruises. They intervened and took custody of our baby. It didn't phase him, not one bit. After going through so much red tape and still not being able to get her, my brother, Paddy and my sister-in-law tried. They were denied. By this time my whole well-being was drained. I emotionally was a wreck and physically looked like one.

One time before all of this, he broke into my step-father's house and threatened Kesah in reference to where I was because he could not find me. Oh, trust me...I tried to leave, but this man walked from South Jersey to North Jersey to find me. If only his determination was geared in the right direction. I dumbly got pregnant again and I knew that I would not emotionally be able to handle social service taking another one of my children. So sadly, I had it terminated. I lied to him as to why I had to get this procedure done just so he would not be angry. Please know that I did not want to do that and it broke me to pieces, but for my peace and my sanity, I had to. I pray God forgives me. My heart was so broken. I was broken.

Then one day, looking out of the window, I saw him walking with this chic. For some reason, that gave me the strength that I needed to leave, as if I opened up a can of spinach with my forearm. We ended up tussling and fighting in the lobby. It was a wrap!! I called the police and had him arrested, then I left to go and stay with my biological father. I just thank God that although I did not know God at the time, He knew me. He kept me through that whole relationship…the physical, the emotional and the verbal abuse. There is so much more to this story, but like I said before, I do not wish to go back down that emotional road. Today, I forgive him. I don't know what he was wrestling with inside at the time…what demons he was trying to fight...but my forgiveness is mostly for me, not for him. I needed to move on and I couldn't do that while holding that in my heart and mind.

If I could give any of these young girls advice, it would be, (1) how a man treats his mother is how he treats the lady in his life. (2) If he is spoiled, by his mom or family, he will expect the same treatment from you. Last but not least, if a man puts his hands on you and you let it slide, believe me, it will happen again. Some women who were in my predicament were not able to live and tell their story. Their significant-other shushed them in one way or another, so I am ever so grateful to not just be telling mine but writing it. There but for the grace of God go I.

# 5 | The Struggle Is Real

After the great ordeal with Mr. Man, I moved into the YWMCA. This place was no better but at least he wasn't there. It was a place for homeless people to go and lay their heads. After being there for some time, I met a friend. She helped me find a job…A barmaid! If you are keeping up with time and my age, no I am not 21…I was only 20. She lied and told the manager I was 21. He hired me right on the spot. I had no idea what I was doing, but I was making a little bit of money. I do admit, I loved the attention that came with the job. How hard was it to pour alcohol and juice in a glass??

Coming back to the YWMCA late, I got to meet the security guard there. We got to know each other and over some time, we started talking. We called ourselves being in a relationship…yep, a false one. He was a big, dark-skinned man. He looked like a bouncer or something in that nature. I have no clue how it happened, but I got pregnant…smart huh? I had no place to stay and nowhere to turn. By the time I was four months pregnant, my time was up at the Y, and apparently up as a barmaid. So now here I am pregnant, I had no job and no one to call. I was staying with that friend that I had met at the Y. I knew I could not stay long. She lived in a two-bedroom apartment and had four children. I had only me. I did call my sister, Wennie, but what good did it do? I ended up going to one of Wennie's friend's cousins' house. That sounds so unreal, but if you know the people, you can follow it. Really…it's true. I stayed with the family up until my 3rd trimester.

They decided that it was time for them to move. They said that for my safety, I should stay behind at her sister's house so that I wouldn't give birth on the side of the road. (like there are hospitals everywhere, right?) But anyway, a month later…yeah…she was late Lol. I gave birth to a beautiful bouncy baby girl! I named her Maliah (Ma-leyah). Maliah was born on September 21st, 1990 in Hartford, CT. We stayed with the lady's sister and we slept on her floor. I didn't have much and neither did my baby. I believed I smelled her so much she had no smell on her by the time she turned a week old. At two weeks old, my baby and I were on the bus to head back to Wennie's house. Still no pot to piss in and no window to throw it out of.

After going back and forth between Aunt Tilda's and Wennie's house, we decided it would be best to get a new start and move to North Carolina. We as in me and Wennie. Yes, the same one who thought it was a good idea to send me to Job Corps. Do I detect a bit of hostility? Yes. I cannot help but feel a bit salty over that. Now here we are heading to North Cackalacky not knowing where this is going…but here we go. Lord, we need your protection.

# 6 | Welcome to North Cackalacky

It's a long train ride when you are riding in the middle of the night with a 7-month-old baby. Not to mention, you are going somewhere that you don't know too much about. The train's last stop was Fayetteville, North Carolina at 4:00 a.m.!! My ride was not there!! My cousin from North Carolina was supposed to come and pick us up! Can you say scared?? Where is this man?? I was so frightened. Sitting on the steps of the train station that is closed because it's after hours, holding your baby and two big suitcases and keeping your eyes peeled on any and everything that moved. Finally, after sitting there for about an hour, here he comes. 'Hey Muletta!' Like…hey where were you?!

I was supposed to be going to stay at one of my cousins' houses but she was not home when we got in by train. Long story short, my aunt from North Carolina fell in love with my baby and we didn't make it to my cousin's house. My aunt was a loving woman of God. She would give her last. She loved my mom and she loved us.

She welcomed Maliah and I with open arms. Wide open!! As for me and my house, we will serve the Lord. And we did. Every Sunday, we got up and got dressed and headed for church. I loved when she would sing. Her voice was angelic. I remember one time at church, I got up to give my life to Christ and she led the song, "It's Going To Rain". She was a very gentle loving soul, and I was blessed to have her a part of not just my childhood life but my adulthood life as well. She is and always will be missed.

While staying with them, I got to know a few people and saw a few old friends. I learned a lot of lessons and was very grateful for all of them…the good and the bad. On August 5th, 1991, I moved into my first apartment with my almost 11-month-old baby. My aunt and my uncle helped me get into my first apartment. They also helped me get some furniture. It was a two-bedroom apartment. It took only four months and I was opening my own front door with my key! God is Faithful.

# 7 | And Baby Makes 3, Then 4

Maliah had her 1st birthday celebration in our apartment. Now, I am on my own. What am I going to do? Still no job, but I do have a pot and a window. It was a bit lonely with just me and her, but we managed with food, snacks and a TV. The bare necessities of a young adult and a baby. SMH

Time had passed, and by then, Maliah had met some friends in the apartment complex and so did I. Some were related so to speak and that made me feel a little more comfortable about staying there. Soon I met a guy…yes, another one. Being that East Arcadia was so close-knit and everyone knew everyone and/or was related to one another, I had to make sure that this guy was not a relative, not even a distant one. I'm just saying. He was from New Jersey, so that was something that we had in common, but no relation. Any who…I met him through one of my male cousins that used to drop by and check up on me. To me, this dude was cute and kind of hoodlike, so the bad boy exterior caught my eye. Maybe I should have met him with my eyes closed. He was orange but brown, resembling a dirty carrot, so that's what I nicknamed him: Dirty Carrot. We talked and got to know each other better and decided, 'Hey, let's get together', and we did.

He made me smile and he made me laugh. I felt safe and secure with him, but I'm thinking today, maybe I should have just rented a comedy movie. Every time he would come in my presence, my heart would drop and melt. I would light up like a Christmas tree and sometimes I felt like I couldn't move. Yes, and unfortunately, I fell in love with this man. I didn't know him as much as I wanted to. Maybe I should have waited and did some type of research…but naw…my silly butt believed your past is just that…your past and not your present or future. I had my doubts, but I didn't let them lead me. But then…can someone say, 'But then?'

I did not know that Mr. Dude was Mr. Player. He was juggling several chics at once. I did not know this at the time. Unfortunately, I was one of them chics! After about a year, Mother Stork came to visit and once again I was with a child. Birth control is not all it's cracked up to be. Although still no job for me, I gave birth to a beautiful bouncing baby girl, and I named her Ja She' (Jashay). She was named after her father.

Born November 5th, 1993, Ja She' was my only on time baby. She was a good baby. By the time she was two months, she was sleeping all night. She must have sensed that her mommy needed some rest. Shay was orange and had big brown eyes that you could swim in. She was my baby dirty carrot. She was a very curious baby, and at a young age loved animals. Now it is me, Maliah and Ja She'.

Mr. Dude didn't lose touch with us and was always there to check on us or stay a night or two. I tried to not let my guard down. You know...I didn't want to get hurt. I always considered our relationship to be a bit complicated. Of course it's complicated when there are more than two people being part of your relationship. We have been through so much stuff. Even though I gave you a timeline in between the things that happen, it was so much of back and forth and to and fro. Him going back and forth, to and fro. Me being an idiot, waiting. I thought our relationship was not going to survive that, but to my surprise, it surpassed it. Way pass, that in May of 1995, we gave birth to our son; James Hayes III. Trey, as we call him, was my first and only son. He favored Uncle Fester when he was a baby. I used to call him that. He had so much energy as a little boy, one of his aunts nicknamed him Tigger. That name fitted him perfectly.

In August 1995, to keep myself busy, I decided to go back to college. I attended a community college and graduated May 1997 with an Associate's Degree in Administrative Office Technology. That was a great accomplishment, graduating from college with three little children. Nobody but God! I worked in the office of the college to gain office experience while going to school. I became good friends with the head person on the campus. We became more than good friends…more like family.

In 1997 on a Saturday morning, I have no idea what happened, but Mr. Dude was acting rather awkwardly. It seemed as if the lights were on but nobody was home. A family friend had taken him to the hospital after his episode and they put him on medication. After that, we didn't see him for a while. They say if you want to make God laugh, tell him your plans. He surely laughed at mine. I have a hunch on what happened but no concrete proof. Things seemed to change with my baby's daddy. He started having strange behavior. All I know is that my children's dad was going in and out of mental hospitals, and for what? I did not know or understood at the time. While he was staying with his family at the time, me and the kids would go and visit him, but he was not himself. His medicines were not regulated and he was out of it most of the time. After quite some time passed, and they had regulated my children's father's medicines, he came back to stay with us. Things were not normal, but they were better. He qualified for help and received it. It helped all of us, so to speak. I am not going to say that things were easy, because we all know that it's not, but I am going to say that it all was worth it. Later, I discovered that he was diagnosed with paranoid schizophrenia. Wow!! What a punch in the gut!! That didn't stop me from loving him. To me, he was still my children's dad and the guy I fell in love with. When all else fails, give it to God.

# 8 | The Drama

After a year had passed, I was eventually told by a close friend of ours that Mr. Dude had pretended to have a psychotic episode so that the judge would not make him pay child support. His intentions were, to me, selfish. They were to only get out of paying for support. So, whatever funding he qualified for, they belonged to him. Like I said, if you want to make God laugh, tell him your plans. He also sees your heart. The one thing about some medicines is that once they get into your system, if there is nothing wrong with you, then there will be. Taken over time, you eventually earn the disability payments they give you.

After hearing this I was so hurt, mad and angry. I had no reason to not believe this person. They had never lied to me before and had nothing to gain by telling me. So, now I had to make a decision on what to do. I decided to allow this man to take care of us.

Tick tock...more time. By this time, I began to feel like something was missing in my life. I felt empty. I began going to church with a neighbor. I started with prayer nights and bible study and then I was going every Sunday. My attendance was so immaculate that when I decided to join the church, they thought I was already a member.

I gave my life to God and was baptized September 8th, 2001. My mother's birthday became my 'Reborn' day. I attended this church for four years. Maliah and Trey were a part of the church as well. They both were in the children's choir and they both were junior ushers. I taught Sunday school for a while. The children from the church made it an enjoyable adventure and learning experience.

Because of my newfound faith, it conflicted with the life I was living. I talked it over with my babies' daddy about not being able to get into heaven straddling the fence, meaning you have knowledge of God but you're still attached to the world and afraid to let go. I wanted to let go. So, either we were going to marry or we were going to leave each other alone because I was ready and it was time to let go.

Through all of that he must have understood to some degree because when asked if he was planning on going to some event in a different state with friends, he told them he will be busy getting married that weekend. Some proposal huh?? Mr. Romantic! So, a date was confirmed. We were married May 20th, 2005.

I then became Mrs. James S. Hayes II. What God has joined together let no man put asunder.

# 9 | He Sustains Me

At the time we were married, I had my own place and he had his in Wilmington, North Carolina. Although my place was bigger, we decided to move to give the kids a better life and to have a bigger place with better opportunities. We didn't move far…just 30 minutes to Wilmington. We made this decision to better ourselves and the kids.

I enjoyed being a mother and a wife. I enjoyed cooking, baking and cleaning. I know it sounds crazy, but I did. Unfortunately, when we moved, I didn't find another church home. As a result, I was not being fed spiritually like I should have been. I blame myself for not reaching out. There are a lot of churches in Wilmington. I was spiritually lost. I don't know what made me stay away so long. I mean, I visited a few churches, but I was not focused. I guess I was suffering a bit from church-hurt. The church that I had belonged to prior sent me a letter stating that if I were not to show up the following Sunday, our membership would be revoked.

Really?? Isn't this God's house? I'm just saying. Needless to say, we didn't go and felt unwanted. Later, I found out that they regretted sending those letters out to people. I forgave them and visited from time to time. It was always a pleasure seeing familiar faces.

We lived in a three-bedroom house with a partially fenced backyard so the kids could play outside. They never did. They only went in the backyard when it was time to rake the leaves or cut the grass. The struggle is real when your income is so low. We struggled but did not starve and were never homeless. Still had that pot and window. God's grace and mercy kept us.

There were a lot of memories in that house. We stayed there for nine years. For nine years, I had no church home but longed for one. Yes, I visited a couple of places, but when I walked through the doors, I didn't like how I felt. You do get some type of feeling when you walk through the doors of a church.

It's so amazing at how we as mothers can actually hide our emotions. We should have been called chameleons. We hide better than they do. I know I did. My hiding got interrupted when we were blessed with our first grandson.

Maliah gave birth to a bouncing baby boy on January 8th, 2012 to Mr. Cameron Jones. For a while I was happy, content and trying to be Grandma. But then the seasons changed and now we are in a whirlwind.

I lost Muletta again. It was an emotional roller coaster. In the same year, 2012, Vonnie lost her husband in April then Paddy passed away unexpectedly in his sleep on May 2nd. He was only 47. Let me tell you a bit about my brother, Paddy. Walk with me a bit down memory lane. Paddy was a serious clown. He was handsome and loved to joke around. He was lost in his teenage years but found himself when he joined the army. He lived with one of my uncles on our mom's side and my uncle treated him like he was his own son. Paddy always treated me with nothing but respect. I wish I had more time with him. When he left this earth, I was lost…so very lost. At the funeral, Aunt Tilda actually held me because I couldn't keep it together. Then only a month and a half later, on June 22nd, she passed away. Now who was going to hold me?

Let's talk about my aunt for a minute. I just want you to know that this is growth right here!! There was a time you couldn't mention her or her name to me. Needless to say, I did not take her death very well. My aunt was very old fashioned. She was, you know, the housewife…dinner on the table by a certain time…a June Beaver so to speak. She was a very good cook. She wasn't really good at affection, but you knew she loved you. We had to sneak kisses and sometimes her hugs were quick. When I moved away, I guess she missed me. Like, really missed me. I say that because her hugs got longer and I actually got kisses!! She was my aunt, 2nd mother, counselor, sound board, advisor, cheerleader, coach. She was my main supporter, my encourager. I have read just about every poem I have written for her to critique. Every time I would read something, her answer would be, "sounds good to me." I bet if I would have written something awful, she still would have said the same thing. I mean this lady knew me so well, she knew my bra size and I was grown with three kids. I love her soooo much. I miss her sooo much!

Like I said, I didn't take her death very well. I was angry, hurt, lost, confused and alone. It started when I went to New Jersey to say goodbye as she was placed in hospice. It felt like my heart was placed in one of those devices and someone was squeezing it so tightly. I didn't want to work on her obituary, and I didn't feel like writing a poem. I just wanted to scream! Yell! I was mad that she left me and she didn't even say goodbye. I felt like I was a little girl and was throwing a tantrum for my aunt. The only thing it was, was an inside tantrum. I was so distraught and didn't know where I could even begin to turn to. I know that my cousins lost their mom, but I lost another mother.

I was depressed to the point where I didn't want to take my medicine. I didn't care what happened to me anymore. I was numb for quite some time. I became a professional at hiding my pain, my fears, my anxiety, my insecurities and mostly my cries at night. Can someone please call a therapist?!! I know for a fact that the only one that heard them was God. James always was sleep, and he sleeps hard. I used to cry and my pillow would be drenched with tears. I still cry but my tears now are wiped before they even fall from my face. I have learned how to control my emotions a bit and to focus on the happier times, but not get so lost in them that I forget I still have to live. But God! He sustains me.

# 10 | The Center of My Vision

Time passes by so quickly. One day, you are
feeding your children at the table and helping with
homework, and the next day, you are saying goodbye at the
front door because they want to go out with friends. I never
thought that I would have empty nest syndrome, but I guess
I do. My kids grew up so fast. Well, not really. Time just
flew by, and before I knew it, my house became empty.
Middle school, high school, proms, games, JROTC,
graduations are all just a memory now. Now it's just me
and Mr. Me. I felt myself falling into a rut. I didn't like who
I was becoming. I started welcoming depression and
lovelessness.

In January of 2013, James had a heart attack.
Thank God it was not a real bad one. I was just diagnosed
with gout and this happened shortly afterwards. He
complained about something being stuck in his chest.
What was happening was his chest was feeling tight. I took
him to the emergency room and after a couple of tests they
determined that he had an attack on his heart.

They inserted a stent in his chest to help and it did. We both changed our diet, and by doing so, his cholesterol dropped immensely. It came down to 140 from a whopping 350. Thank you, Lord, for Grace!

Because of the emptiness and the cardiac episode, we decided that it would be best to move from our house to an apartment. It would require low maintenance, therefore less stress for me and him. We also included a pet...a companion. A cute little black and white puppy mixed with part-lab and part-pit. Someone should have warned us how big them labs get. We got Bryan when he was two months old. His name is Bryan because he looks like a dog from one of my favorite shows. Bryan quickly became a part of the family. He thinks he is one of our children.

One evening in 2014, one of my associates called and asked if I would like to go with her to bible study at this new church she heard of. I told her sure. We pulled into a funeral parlor and so many questions ran inside my head. My first question was...did she know where she was going? And the next question was, do I have to use the ladies room? No...good because once I was seated, there was no moving for me until it was time to leave. To my surprise, I really enjoyed bible study. I even started going on my own without my associate.

I loved the pastor there and loved the people. I felt comfortable. I learned so much. It was more than likely because it was broken down to us. I started going to Sunday School and Sunday service. The pastor preached as they taught, and more importantly, taught as they preached. I loved that and learned quite a lot. I loved learning. I even started taking notes and going back to writing poetry again.

In February 2015, it became an official church, so I joined this new beginning church. After being there for a good minute, the pastor asked what my gift was. I answered, poetry. So, they made room for it. A poetry ministry was established at our church, and I recited a poem every Sunday. Sometimes I would take notes from the sermon before and revamp them and create a poem from the notes. I would do that also when we went away to other churches. Of course, I would look it up in the bible to confirm what I wrote. So, in a way, my poetry helped me study God's Word.

I recited at women's conferences, men's conferences and other churches. My praying became different. I started asking God what He would like for me to say to His people. God was speaking to me through my poetry. I would wake up in the middle of the night and verses would play in my mind like a song you can't get out of your head. It would play over and over until I got up and wrote it down. Sometimes it would be a verse or two and other times it would be a whole poem. I would wake up the next day and read what I wrote and just cry because I was so in awe. I love how God uses me. Sometimes I cried because my God is just so awesome! During my membership, I wore the hats of usher, armor bearer and secretary. I loved the assignments that were handed to me and tried my best to fulfill them.

Once again, we suffered a loss. In July 2016, I lost one of my good friends. She was like a sister to me. We would disagree sometimes, but I knew regardless, she always had my back. I also knew that she genuinely loved me and my family. I miss her so much. From time to time, I would pull out either or both the poem I wrote for her and her obituary just to read it or look at her. We talked about everything. She looked out for me when things happened in the neighborhood. She was an encourager, a friend and a sister to me. She didn't like to eat alone, so we always went to lunch. I was blessed for the time that I did have with her.

On January 4th, 2017, once again, God blessed Maliah with a bouncing baby girl. She named her Aaliyah Naomi Skye. Yes, after the singer and my friend. After four years of belonging to this church, I heard God say it was time for me to leave. I became stagnant in my poetry ministry and in everything else. My focus was blurred, and I knew it was time for a shift. I was feeling like this for quite some time, but of course, I waited until God told me to go.

Six months before I left, I started attending another church at the same time. Yes, I would attend two services every Sunday. Sometimes Maliah would join me. It was located right across from us and was very easy to just leave our church and go there. When I first started going...oh my goodness. I didn't know what to think. When I walked in the door I felt so loved and so welcomed. I mean, members would just wave like they knew me forever. I am smiling as I write this because I can still feel the warmness of their genuine love. I felt God's presence all throughout their sanctuary. It felt peaceful and serene. So, January 2020, I joined their church.

# 11 | *Don't Be Afraid Of The Shift*

## (It's Time To Get Uplifted and Increase My Faith)

Although I was going through quite a bit at the time, so was Maliah. Maliah actually joined the new church first. I was so surprised. I then joined in January 2020…the beginning of Covid. I had it the December before, right after my birthday and don't remember the new year coming in. I thank God for how he has kept me. The first Sunday after my membership, it was spoken over my life for me not to be afraid of the shift. Little did I know how much of a shift would take place. The members were all accepting, and I felt love every time I came through the door. It was like old family members that you have not seen in a good minute. It was only a week, but the excitement was still there.

I began reading my poetry on the regular and they did not applaud, they snapped their fingers. Lol I thought that was neat. Did I say neat?? That sounds so cheesy and corny. I didn't want to be one of those members that sat way, way back and felt out of touch with everything.

I wanted to sit in the middle so I can focus on what God had to say. But of course, my seat was at the back of the church. That is where I sat every Sunday.

During the Covid pandemic, I had no idea how I was going to minister to people because we were not doing too much or going to many places. Everything was basically closed or limited. Can you say, 'But God.??' Before the end of the year came to pass, in the middle of a pandemic, God had blessed me and allowed me to have my first book of poems published. It was entitled, "Inspirational Poetry: To Prick Your Heart, Convict Your Soul and Renew Your Mind". Some of the poems in this book were written so much earlier in my life. Remember, I was writing for a long time. Plus, at my previous church, I was writing basically every week. Look at God!!

I was ministering to people through my writing. It was my apostle's idea to have a book signing at our church. My church family was so supportive. I cannot begin to explain to you how full I was. The majority of the books that I had with me were purchased by my church family. I had mixed emotions. I was extremely happy of course, but at the same time, I was sad because my aunt was not here to celebrate with me. She would have been overjoyed and probably would have bought a dozen books. Yes, my aunt…my number one cheerleader! I am certain that she celebrated in heaven. My first book sold over 50 copies before it was even offered online. Not only that, but it also sold overseas making me an international author!! I was on Cloud 9.

Now it was time to grind again and continue working on my second book. This was a big deal to me. Over the past years, I had been promised so many things in reference to getting my book published that I almost stopped believing in myself and allowing the enemy to convince me that it couldn't be done. So, instead of talking to people, I turned and talked to God. At the time I was not working, so I prayed and asked him to touch someone's heart to help me get my book published. Wayen had given me the name of a beginning publisher that would publish my book, but I still needed the funds. After about a week talking to God, an old friend and I were on the phone. They said, "I don't know why, but I am going to help you financially get your book published." I started crying because I knew why. And they helped. I thank God for touching their heart and I thank them for their help. God is so faithful!!

In October of 2021, my second book was birthed. It's entitled, "Poetry In Motion: Moving Forward To The Next Level". Still no job, but God is still faithful. The same friend that helped me last time helped me again partly. I was excited about this book as well. BOOK #2!! Same thing: I did a book signing at my church, sold more than 50 copies before it even got to the internet and sold internationally as well. I decided after that to take a break and start again the following year on book number three. For those who are lost in counting…this is book number three. It was time to change my focus back on my purpose. I didn't lose it, I just focused on something else instead of poetry.

In between those years of the publishing of my books so much has happened. Tragically, on November 20th, 2020, my sister, Wennie, fell out of a three-story window. We don't know all the preliminaries, but what we do know is that it was a life gone too soon. She was only 57 at the time. Let me shed some light on this beautiful soul. Wennie was 12 when my mother passed away. Just about to hit her teen years, a time when most little girls needed their mother. She tried her very best to keep all of us together. She and Paddy would pick me up and we would head to Kesah's house.

Although it was not the best life a person could ask for, she still graduated from Penn State University in the top 20 of her class. She was a 7th grade teacher and loved kids. She was fighting battles that we may never understand. I was so proud of her for all her achievements and all that she had overcome thus far. She was a bright star and her intelligence was far beyond measurement. I have so many questions and not enough answers. I know my mother was waiting in the midst with open arms for both of them. They will be forever missed and forever in our hearts. My little sister and I are the last siblings of Mrs. Hattie B. King.

My little sister is so loving and gentle and mean all wrapped up in one. She doesn't take any mess. She is the sister you call upon as you're growing up to approach that bully. When she loves, she loves hard and gives you her best. She is smart and highly intelligent. She loves her family. At the time of this writing, she is married and has two boys of her own. I wish I lived closer. I wish that all the time. I said I wouldn't mention names in my book, but I cannot let it go without shouting out to my sister, LaKeisha!!! From cradle to grave…womb to tomb…I love you more than you will ever know. To the moon and back wrapped around 15 million times over momma! Little joke there. She has the habit of calling some of us momma.

Now it was time to refocus, rejuvenate and restore. At the beginning of 2022, I wanted to be not just a more active member, but I wanted to be an effective member, so I took classes at my church. I did at least four or five sermonettes. I wanted to learn as much as I could learn. With my classes, I learned so much about who my God is and who I am. My desire was to do better and to be better. So, with each passing day, that was my goal.

In October 2022, my heart was broken once more. You see, Arnie's wife decided that it was time for her to go home. She came into our lives shortly after my mom passed away. They, in turn, were married. She claims I did not like her, nor would I even eat her food when I first met her. I told her, "Give me a break, I was only 7." But over the years I have gotten really close to her. The last four years were even closer. I would call and talk to her at least three or more times a day. Although she was going through so much and was in so much pain, she made time for me. I couldn't imagine my life without her. I shared everything with her. When she talked to me and told me that she was going to stop dialysis, I asked her, "You know what's going to happen, right?" She replied, "Yes." I then asked, "What am I supposed to do without you?" Gently and softly, she replied, "Live." I am so glad and thank God that I went to visit her that June. When it was time for me to leave, my soul did not want to go and now I know why. She made me laugh and cheered me up and on. She was and always will be a part of my heart. Rest in heaven, Chickie.

I continued my studies. I am waiting for God to bless me with my own language so that I too can talk to him. Not that I can't talk to him now, but it's a powerful thing to have your own language that you can relate to God with. Oh, I desire a closer relationship with God. One of my pastors asked me to take another class and I agreed. It was to become a Deaconess. I was ordained in January of 2024.

I am having a longing. Sometimes it scares me, and other times I feel at peace. How can I explain this where even a child could understand?? When Jesus returns, I want to be ready and go with him. I don't want to be left here on this earth. I beg him every chance I get, please God, let me be ready. Do what you must do to prepare me to be in your kingdom. I will do what you want me to do, I will go where you want me to go, I will say what you want me to say but let me be ready. It's time to get uplifted and increase my faith.

# Please Don't Leave Me Here God

Please don't leave me here God
I want a seat in your kingdom with your son
Oh, to be at your Holy feet
and hear you say, well done

Search my heart, oh Lord
and if there is anything not of you
I ask that you cleanse me now
so that your love may shine through

As we are divided apart
let me not be in despair
But know without a shadow of doubt
that I too will meet you in the air

Oh, wonderful Savior
Lord of Lords...King of Kings
Draw me closer to thee
as I sought out my heavenly wings

I am in desperation
for I know and feel the time is near
I want to be ready
when you in all your glory reappear

I humble myself to thee
before the first trumpet blows
I lay myself upon the altar
surrendering it all from my head to my toes

Please dear Father in heaven
don't let it be too late
When you come for your bride
let me be ready to meet you at the gate

Don't leave me here, dear God
your Word I shall impart
I, now as Hannah did
pour out from my aching heart

Clean me up, fix me, mold me
whatever you must do
So, when the day comes
I will be ready to be with you

We are in the latter days
I believe this to be true
I pray for strength and guidance
until I am safe with you

Please don't leave me Father
with you I so desperately long to be
A seat in your heavenly kingdom
with anticipation, I will wait on thee.

# 12 | Pushed Into Your Purpose

As I sit and wait on God, I have acquired a job at a local nursing home. First, let me share with you how I acquired this position. My apostle sent a group text out to let everyone who is interested in a receptionist position know about the position available. I privately texted her back. She gave me a phone number to call. I called and I got called in for an interview.

At the interview, they were explaining to me my duties and responsibilities for the job. I was like 'oh my!' It was extremely overwhelming. I was very polite and courteous during the interview and did not let them see me sweat. I knew deep down inside that I could not handle all that was required of me. I was just getting myself back in the work world from a long stay at home. In no way was I going to survive that type of juggling. So, I began to pray. *Lord, I need them to have a part-time position. You know I need a job and I am willing to work. You also know what I can bear.* Not even a month later they called me back. They had a part time position available where I could work evenings every day and every other weekend. They just wanted me to work the morning hours until they had a chance to train another woman who would be the day receptionist. Hallelujah!! Won't God Do It!!!!!!!

The work I do here is very easy and simple. I answer the phones and help with some of the residents, making sure that the ones who are not allowed outside don't go. I also help with some of the daytime duties if she is overwhelmed and needs assistance. Honestly speaking, I do not believe that I was sent here to actually do the work of a receptionist which I was hired for. I'm sitting here working on my book and I also work on my sermonettes sometimes.

While doing research for one of my sermonettes, which is supposed to be about bearing fruit in a difficult season, I was focusing on the fruits in which to bear. As I looked over my notes and read them, I began to cry. I realized that I have been bearing fruit at my job from day one of working here. I have bared every fruit of the spirit in some way or fashion. Isn't that awesome??!! Not just to residents of the facility, but to faculty and visitors as well. I love my job and how I feel when I leave work. I believe that it is a blessing to be able to spread love and encouragement wherever you go. No matter how hard you may have it, just know there is someone out there who would do anything to trade places with you. There is no problem too big that God cannot fix. I have learned to lean on him and give it all to him. I can't do anything with it.

My life at home has been somewhat a bit stressful. Although my kids are grown, you never stop being a mother. I don't really believe that I am loved, respected or even cared for. I don't feel a connection like I did when they were little, and even though I feel that way, it still does not stop me from being a mom. I used to say that my name was Annette because I was always there to catch them when they fell. A Net!! Now some of you may say to yourselves as you are reading this, 'well Muletta, that is what you are supposed to do!' No ma'am! I am not supposed to be used by any children that I brought into this world. That was not on my mother card.

I am just functioning. I just exist. It feels like my brain is going to and from, but at the same time, staying still. My husband likes to talk to himself. Excuse me… "sort things out". He does that a lot. He wears headphones in his ears all the time. Yes…even in bed. At first, I made sure he had them on. I did not want him to be outside talking to himself and some stupid idiot thinks that he is talking to him and starts some mess with my husband, or worse, want to fight. And you know people nowadays do not fight fair. But it is scary to think that if something happens in the house, he would not be able to hear me. That is very aggravating. It is also aggravating when you are trying to spend some time with someone and they'd rather "sort things out."

So, there it is…my family. I just don't like the way I have been feeling lately. I don't like the way I have been treated lately. I don't like a lot of things that have been going on lately. So, I guess I need to do something about it. Pray. I know that God will sustain me. He promised me in his Word to never leave me nor forsake me. I am leaning and depending on Him and ONLY Him. He is my refuge. Every time God is about to elevate you, the enemy tries his best to distract you. That is basically what was happening. But I see you, devil. You get NO ACCESS here!! I had to pray even more…for me and my family. My convocation was January 13, 2024. I was ordained as Deaconess Muletta Hayes. What an honor and a privilege to be a worker in God's house. And now, I just sit and wait for God to let me know what he will have me do next. Oh, to be used by God…

# 13 | Testimonials

Sometimes when we go through stuff, we literally go through stuff and it feels as if you are screaming trapped in a soundproof room because no one hears you. Your mind starts playing games on you, leading you to believe that they hear you but just don't care. My mind did that quite a lot. It made me believe that my family did not care, my husband did not care, and yes, my children did not care. So, while going through that, I began not to care. I mean why should I have cared? No one else did. But, I realized that I was the most important person to care, even if no one else cared. I lost control and had to regain it back.

As I look back over my life, I can see where God stepped in. I remember the first time hearing him speak to my heart. It was in 2001, before I was baptized. He spoke to my heart and told me to go and bless a member of our church with groceries. I received benefits at the time and my children and I went to the store to buy food. On our way back, I kept hearing God speak to my heart. We got home and put the groceries away. Still, God was talking.

So, I told the kids I will be right back. Don't be ridiculous; I got someone to watch them. I proceeded to the woman's house. I told her that God told me to come and get her and take her to get some groceries. I needed to be obedient. Being the God-fearing woman that she was, she got in my car and we headed to the store. On our way, she kept glancing at me as I was crying and driving. When we got to the store, I told her to get whatever she needed and don't worry about the cost. I paid for her groceries and then I took her home and helped her put her things away. She thanked me and I left. I did not know she was in need, but God did. Neither one of us spoke of it again until years later, but I will tell you this…God did not allow my cupboard to go empty or lack. <u>Obedience is better than sacrifice.</u> I am so glad I heard him, and I was obedient.

   I strongly believe in the power of prayer. I have faith and believe that all things are possible to them that believe. I also know that faith without work is dead. When my son got into a bit of trouble and was incarcerated for something he was accused of doing, I was beside myself. I was attending the church that had just become a church at the time, working in the Lord's house and being obedient. My son went to court at least three times, and every time, he was denied to come home. Every time we spoke on the phone, I heard screaming and crying in his voice, but I knew he would never tell me that. He would never want me to worry about him. But I was his mother, so of course I worried. Now, it was time for him to go once again to court. It was also time for me to have a talk with God. I gave God my petition and asked that my son come home. I didn't care if he was on house arrest where he couldn't even leave my front porch, I just wanted him home with me where he was safe. I reminded God of his promises to me, and with tears rolling down my face, I poured out everything that I had till I was almost out of breath. That night I slept. The next day was court. As I went in, I felt something different. I looked and there was a different judge. The atmosphere was different. The smell of the hallway was different. My outlook was different. But God, was and still will be the same. That day, that judge sent my baby home. Can you say, "Glory to God?!" It took me just 15 minutes to get to the jail, crying and praising God all the way there. I was so excited and relieved that I didn't realize that I had to wait for them to bring him back from the courthouse. God is faithful!

When God steps in, he steps in. One time, I was suffering from pain in my little girl's spot. I didn't know what was going on. All I knew was that it hurt badly. I was in my 40's at the time. I went to the doctor, and they told me I had a mass 5 cm long and 2 cm wide. They said I had to get it surgically removed. If you know me, you know I do not want to be put to sleep. My surgery was scheduled for two days later. I cried out to God and told him if this surgery was not for me, please do not allow me to have to go through this.

The day of the surgery came and my husband was by my side. They called the anesthesiologist to come and talk to me so I can get prepared for surgery. I began to cry, 'Lord Lord!!' They comforted me and told me that we could just reschedule it for another time. That should tell you how bad I was crying…change that baby's diaper!

A week went by and then I went to my follow up appointment. The same doctor I saw asked me how the surgery went. I was honest with him and told him I didn't have it. He insisted that I did because the mass was not there anymore. GLORY!!!! 5 cm long, 2 cm wide!!! He asked, "If you didn't have the surgery, where did it go?" My response was, "I serve a God who sits high and looks low, who hears my every cry and my every moan." He was in awe, and I must admit, I was too. God always puts me in awe by what he does. He's able!!

## Pushed Into Your Purpose

Everyone who walked away is not a mistake
God knew we couldn't do it without a nudge
For when everything is good, we are comfortable
determined not to move, we won't budge

God has a plan for great purpose
and a beautiful future for all who believe
Not despite our past, but because of it
all we have to do is receive

God uses loss, betrayal and persecution
not for misery, but to force us to change
Pushing you into your purpose
so your life may rearrange

He will use people against you to move you
to try to throw you in the pit, discredit you,
toss at you a stone…
No need to take it personally…you needed your Judas kiss
so that you can take your throne

Your purpose in life is not a one and done
it's not even a destination
It's a glorious journey that requires persistence,
perseverance, and great determination

He can take a test in your life and create a testimony,
a crisis and show Christ all through it
God doesn't waste any experiences you have
any problems you cross, He will break through it

Your destiny belongs to God
He created us to expand, flourish into greatness and grow
Before you were born, your life was written in his book
even if a push is needed, into your purpose you will go.

# 14 | A New Meaning

Muletta - (Malita)

A name that beholds the fitting meaning of 'honey sweet.' A variation of the ancient Greek name, Melite, a sea-nymph who calmed the seas. This name offers both beautiful meanings and amazing imagery.

Meaning: honey-sweet; calm; splendid.

an island in the Mediterranean, the modern Malta. In fact, the ancient name for the island is derived from Phoenician Melita, which means, "refuge."

Acts 28:1 King James Version
*"And when they were escaped, then they knew that the island was called Melita."*

A Sweet Refuge

## Descendants of Muletta Hayes

At the time of this writing, I have 13 wonderful grandchildren. I would not trade any of them for anything. I only put two of them in my writing because I knew it would become exhausting, so I decided to just do a family tree starting from muah.

James Hayes    Muletta Hayes

Ja She' Hayes    James Hayes III   Maliah Dunlap

Se' Maj Hayes    James Hayes IV   Cameron Jones

Myra McAllister    Amaryllis Hayes   Aaliyah Graham

Me Kael McAllister    Lazelle Hayes   Zamiyah Devine

Theodore Hayes    Elijah Devine

Aubrey Hayes

Yana Hayes

# Pain For His Purpose

Psalm 34:17-20 tells us, *"Yes, the Lord hears the good man when he calls to him for help and saves him out of all his troubles. (18) The Lord is close to those whose hearts are breaking; he rescues those who are humbly sorry for their sins. (19) The good man does not escape all troubles—he has them too. But the Lord helps him in each and every one. (20) Not one of his bones is broken. Not even a finger gets broken."*

God uses our pain for his purposes and for our own good. He may allow us to be bruised, but he does not allow us to be broken to the point we cannot be repaired. He gives us what we need and does not allow us to go through unnecessary suffering. He is always near us. He keeps, delivers and saves us. He knows our hearts and he can see our pain. He is just and loving and he redeems the lives of his servants. Whatever bruising we are experiencing at the moment, we take solace in knowing that he is our healer. So, in our pain let's rest and trust in Him, believing he will meet us and bandage our wounds. He can do all things but fail.

# Conclusion

God, I thank you that you do not waste suffering. Thank you for how you were always near to me and how you kept me. Thank You for saving me, for continuing to do so, and for the day when you will fully save me. Help me to surrender my pain and tribulations to you, laying it all at your feet and not picking it back up so that you might give me peace, rest, and trust. In Jesus' name I pray, Amen.

# When God Chooses You

When God chooses you,
he wants someone to walk with, to talk with, for you to be
that one
he wants to share himself with you
for you are a pearl of great price compared to none

When God chooses you,
it's because he loved you before time began
before any stars were burning, any tree was growing, any
stream was flowing,
he gave you destiny before he created anything, including
land

When God chooses you,
he chose you to show you hope
that hope is to one day be like Christ
he called you, saved you, loved you…to be in his image,
the hope of glory and all he sacrificed

When God chooses you,
he chose you to be holy and for him, to be set apart
to represent him in his holiness
and to be pure of heart

When God chooses you,
he chose you to live in fellowship with his only
begotten son
to walk in a friendship and in a partnership
his love for you is paramount, you are his special someone

When God chooses you,
he chose you to live in freedom, and in the heart of God,
move deep
true freedom by allowing him to have all your well-being
not living in fear, knowing and trusting, you, he will keep

When God chooses you,
it's to show the world a unique message that only you
can present
you are his divine poetry…so eloquent
displaying all of his glory to its fullest extent

When God chooses you,

it is all of you, what makes you…you

your life, your unique gifts, your passion for Him

bringing to the world a poetic expression of his love

shining so bright with no chance of dim

How does it feel to be the lyrics of love on two legs

using you for his glory as you put him first

in all that you do,

having the comfort and satisfaction of a blessed life

when God chooses you?

# Are You A Cheerful Giver, Or Are You A Fearful Giver?

Will a man rob God? Yes, in his giving
all belongs to him including gold and silver
Ten percent is all he asks
Are you a cheerful or a fearful giver?

He doesn't ask much of us
but yet, he gave so free
Sacrificed his life on the cross
hung, bled and died for you and me

That position that you carry
that career, that trade, that job
was a blessing and on purpose
So why on your payday it's God you rob?

He blesses our coming in
he blesses our going out
he's Jehovah Jireh, our provider
he continues to bless us, even when we doubt

Some people give so freely
because they know the God they serve
who will bless them abundantly
and give them much more than they deserve

Some people live in fear
their trust and their faith is quite dim
not understanding who their real source is
and that everything belongs to him

Pressed down, shaken together, running over
he promised you will never lack
Whatever measure you use to give
will be used to measure what is given back

When you place your faith in Christ
in time, you will be sowing your seeds
transformed into a giver
realizing who supplies all your needs

It means that through faith
you'll be empowered, knowing God will deliver
not fearful of what you think you will lose
but change into a cheerful giver

Will a man rob God? Yes, in his giving

All belongs to him, including gold and silver

Ten percent is all he asked of you

Are you a cheerful or fearful giver?

# Enough Is Enough

**Genesis 27:40** *"And it shall come to pass, when you become restless, that you shall break his yoke from your neck."*

**Isaiah 52:2** *"Shake yourself from the dust, arise...loose yourself from the bonds of your neck."*

Are you tired of the enemy causing chaos?
Your life upside down, he's all in your stuff...
creating disorder and elevating confusion
and you want to scream...enough is enough!!

If you are at that point...GOOD!!
You're able to throw off the enemy's yolk...
the ones that bind you, the ones that blind you
and the ones that are meant to choke

If things aren't too bad
people tend to endure and tolerate
thinking surely, the Lord understands, which He does
and eventually, He will rehabilitate

However, when they become desperate
as if they were drowning in the sea
they will do whatever is necessary
to break themselves free

God has told us to free ourselves
in Isaiah, it's conferred
He has also given us the means to do it
and that is through his Word

God's Word, The Sword of the Spirit
is an attack weapon; its power...none can deny it
but you can't just read from cover to cover
you need to pick it up and apply it

You have to reach the point of being restless
tired of being bruised, battered and broke
that is when you will rise up and use your authority in Jesus
and throw off the enemy's yolk

Enough is enough today....
it's time to rise up in Jesus' name, who'll see you through
and walk in the freedom
he has already provided for you

So don't be one of the ones

to tolerate the enemy's chaos and all his stuff

grab your sword that God has given to you

and declare, Enough is Enough!!

# She Still Rises

She knows today is a new day
and as this day begins
She vows to take it at it's worth
knowing that again…today…she will win!
She Still Rises

It doesn't matter what anyone may say or think
her purpose, they will never deter
For God told her in his Word
who she is and that he will always be with her

She is saved, not according to her works
but according to His purpose and His grace
She is complete…she is chosen…she is forgiven
and wrapped in His arms with a warm embrace
She Still Rises

She is safe, she is victorious, she is whole
She is free…she is guarded by God's peace
She is redeemed, she is strong, she is blessed
She is loved, overflowing that will never cease
She Still Rises

She is more than a conqueror

She can do all things through Christ who strengthens her

She is the true vine, she is the salt of the earth

She is called to be who He wants her to be—

and not what she prefers

She is accepted, she is beautiful, she is special

She is hopeful, she is joyful and she is wonderfully made

She is healed and she is not alone…she is sufficient

knowing His love for her will never fade

She Still Rises

She is the head and not the tail

She is stronger than she'd ever thought she were

Even in her darkest moments

She knows that God is still with her

So, as this day unfolds

She will be the light that refuses to dim

For she is chosen, holy and blameless before God

She is His child and she belongs to HIM

She still rises and will continue to do so

because she is determined and destined to be

I know all of this to be true

For She is Me…And She Still Rises!!

# About The Author

There is no need for an "About the Author" section because all my information is the book itself. But I can tell you this: while writing this book I have learned so much about myself and saw myself from a different perspective. If I had to do it all over again, yes there are some things I would have done differently, and some things I may have said would not have been said. Like I said, I have learned quite a bit about myself.

My experiences would have been different because the choices I've made would have been different. When you know better, you are supposed to do better. I have tried to implement that in my life. Although I did not know God, I am so glad and grateful that he knew me. He knows my name, my purpose and my destiny. I'm thankful for all he has done, what he is doing right now and all that he is going to do. I know that he is not done with me yet. I'm looking for him to move more in my life than ever before. Until then, I will patiently wait. Thank you for allowing me to share my journey with you.

# Other Titles By Muletta Hayes

"Inspirational Poetry: To Prick Your Heart, Convict Your Soul, & Renew Your Mind" (2020)
Available at www.rdtalleybooks.com

"Poetry In Motion: Moving Forward To The Next Level" (2021)
Available at www.rdtalleybooks.com

www.ingramcontent.com/pod-product-compliance
Lightning Source LLC
Chambersburg PA
CBHW071104120626
46546CB00003B/1267